Golden Retriever

Charles and Linda George

Created by Q2AMedia
www.q2amedia.com
Editor Jeff O' Hare
Publishing Director Chester Fisher
Client Service Manager Santosh Vasudevan
Project Manager Kunal Mehrotra
Art Director Harleen Mehta
Designer Pragati Gupta
Picture Researcher Nivisha Sinha

Library of Congress Cataloging-in-Publication Data
Golden retriever / [Charles George,Linda George].
p. cm. — (Top dogs)
Includes index.
ISBN 0-531-23241-7/ 978-0-531-23241-5 (hardcover)
1. Golden retriever—Juvenile literature. I. Title. II. Series.
SF429.G63G543 2010
636.752'7—dc22
2010035033

This edition published by Scholastic Inc.,

Printed and bound in Heshan, China
232656 10/10
10 9 8 7 6 5 4 3 2 1

Picture Credits
t= top, b= bottom, c= center, r= right, l= left

Cover Page: Joop Snijder jr/Shutterstock.

Title Page: Linn Currie/Shutterstock.

4-5: Micimakin/Shutterstock; 5: Volina/Shutterstock; 6-7: D McKenzie/Shutterstock; 6: Eric Isselée/Shutterstock; 8-9: Naoki Mutai/Photolibrary; 10-11: Richard Semik/Shutterstock; 12-13: Aldo Murillo/Istockphoto; 14-15: Richard Semik/Dreamstime; 16: Tstockphoto/Shutterstock; 16-17: Rolf J Kopfle/Photolibrary; 18-19: David W Hamilton/Photolibrary; 19: Chuck St. John/Photolibrary; 20: Koh Sze Kiat/Shutterstock; 20-21: Stefan Hess/Istockphoto; 22: Sonya Etchison/Shutterstock; 23: Photodisc/Photolibray; 24: Stockbroker/Photolibrary; 25: Photodisc/Photolibrary; 26-27: Linn Currie/Shutterstock; 27: Joop Snijder jr/Shutterstock; 28: Iofoto/Shutterstock; 29: Bob Winsett/Photolibrary; 30: Canine Partners; 30-31: Mark Mainz/Getty Images.

Contents

What are Golden Retrievers?

Everyone loves Golden **Retrievers**. (*ree-tree-vers*). We call them Goldens. They are just like their name, too. They are golden in color. They are smart, friendly, and **loyal**. Goldens make great pets and friends!

Fast Fact

Retrieve is another word for bring back.

People in Scotland and England needed strong hunting dogs. They wanted dogs that loved to swim. They also wanted dogs that would bring back the birds they shot. Golden retrievers were raised for these purposes. They came from other kinds of retrievers and spaniels.

Fast Fact
The first Goldens were raised in Scotland in the 1800s.

Everyone Loves Goldens!

Goldens are best friends with their people. They are **devoted** to their owners. Goldens are polite house dogs. They have lots of energy, but they are very calm.

Fast Fact

Goldens can be too playful. Good training teaches good manners.

Goldens need exercise every day. This keeps them happy and healthy. They are always ready to play. They like to explore. They like playing **fetch**.
They like to carry things in their mouths.

Fast Fact
A perfect day for a Golden is playing fetch on the beach!

Goldens Love Kids!

Goldens make perfect pets. They get along with the whole family. They like children. They don't bite or nip when their tails are pulled. Goldens treat kids like their own puppies.

Fast Fact

Goldens are big, so when they get excited, they may knock over small children.

You and your Golden puppy can grow up together. You will be long-time friends. You can trust your Golden to be gentle and sweet. A Golden is the perfect dog for any size family.

Fast Fact

Because they are so friendly, Golden Retrievers don't make good watchdogs.

Puppy Love!

At birth, Goldens are fairly large puppies. They usually weigh 14 to 18 ounces (0.4-0.5 kg) at birth. Golden puppies are about as long as a hot dog bun. They weigh about the same as a can of soda.

Fast Fact

Golden puppies grow fast. They can be cute and clumsy, too.

Not all Golden Retrievers are the same color. Most have **coats** that are pale gold. They can also be blond. Some can be darker.

Fast Fact
Some Goldens have such a deep golden coat that they look almost rust-colored.

11

Choosing a Golden Retriever Puppy

Choosing a Golden puppy is like picking one nugget from a box of gold! Choose the puppy you like best. It will be the puppy who likes you best, too!

Fast Fact

Golden puppies are born in **litters** of six to ten.

If you are not sure which puppy to pick, wait a little bit. See which puppy comes to you. Friends know each other, even in a crowd!

Fast Fact

Newborn Golden puppies don't open their eyes for at least a week after they're born. This is normal.

Taking Care of Your Golden

Golden puppies need a warm, dry place to sleep. After they stop **nursing** from their mother, they can eat puppy food. Don't feed them table food. It isn't good for them. They also need clean, cool water to drink.

Fast Fact

Give your puppy treats when you train it.

A Golden's coat can be wavy or smooth. Its **undercoat** is the fuzzy fur that grows close to its skin. This fur keeps the Golden warm when the temperature turns cold.

Fast Fact

Goldens can live outside, even in cold climates. They are happier living inside with their people.

How Big do Goldens Get?

Adult male Goldens weigh between 65 and 75 pounds (29.5-34 kg). They are 23-24 inches (58.4-61 cm) tall. Female Goldens are a little smaller. They weigh between 55 and 65 pounds (25-29.5 kg). Female Goldens are 21-23 inches (53.3-58.4 cm) tall.

Fast Fact

When an adult Golden stretches out, it can cover a sofa!

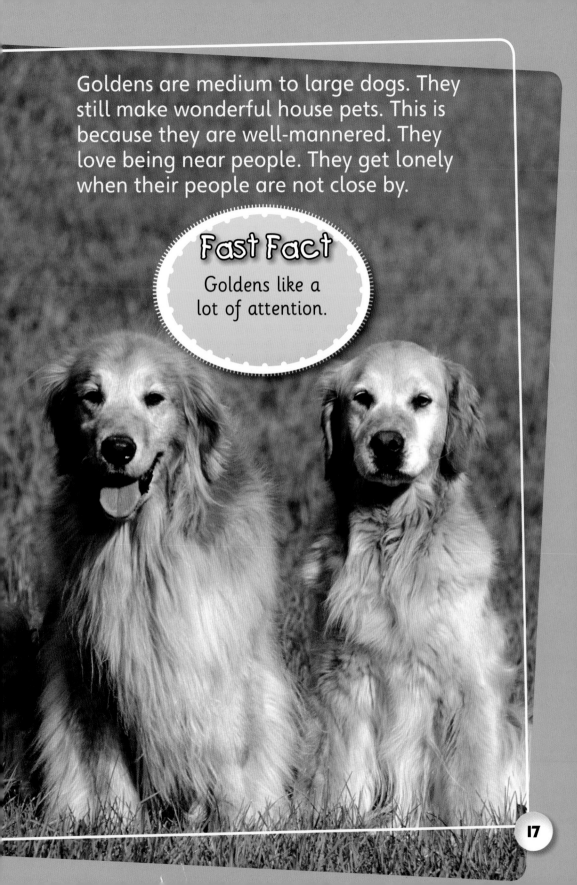

Goldens are medium to large dogs. They still make wonderful house pets. This is because they are well-mannered. They love being near people. They get lonely when their people are not close by.

Fast Fact

Goldens like a lot of attention.

Brushing Hair and Clipping Nails

A Golden has long hair. It should be brushed two times a week. The dog's nails should be trimmed when they get ragged. A veterinarian, also called a vet, is a pet doctor. Ask your vet to trim your Golden's nails.

Fast Fact

A Golden's coat is longer than the coat of a Labrador Retriever.

Take your Golden to the vet at least once a year. The vet will give your dog a check-up. Your dog also needs shots every year, to keep it healthy.

A Dog as Good as Gold

Golden Retrievers are very active. They love to be busy. They like to work, and they like to play. They enjoy running, swimming, or exploring new places.

Fast Fact
Goldens love to be in the water.

Goldens can be quiet, too. They like to sit beside their owners after a long day of work or play. They also like to sleep near their owner's feet.

Fast Fact

Goldens love the outdoors! They will enjoy going camping or hiking with you!

Make Room for Your Golden!

If your house is small, a Golden may not be the best dog for you. A Golden needs room to walk, run, and play. It will like a home with a big backyard. You can take your Golden for a walk on a **leash**, too.

Fast Fact

Goldens get along fine with other dogs. If you live in a city, check out the nearest **dog park**.

A Golden does best as an indoor dog. A Golden can also live outside in a fenced yard. Can your Golden get out of the sun when it's hot? Does it have a warm place to sleep when it's cold? That's perfect!

Fast Fact

A good game to play with your Golden is tug-of-war.

So Smart!

Golden Retrievers are easy to train. They want to please you by doing what they are told.

Golden Retrievers are very smart dogs. They know how you are feeling.Do you feel silly and want to play? They'll play with you! Are you sad and need a friend? Goldens are good friends when you feel sad.

A Golden helps people by being a good friend. People who live alone may like having a dog as a friend. A Golden is perfect for them. A Golden keeps them company when they feel lonely.

Fast Fact

At the San Diego Zoo, Goldens are friends for other animals! One Golden is friends with a big cat called a **cheetah**!

25

Wonderful Hunters

Golden Retrievers were raised to be hunting dogs. They aren't afraid of gunfire. They are strong and can carry heavy birds when retrieving. Their sense of smell helps them find the animals.

Fast Fact

Golden retrievers came to the U.S. around 1912.

A Golden can be trained to sniff out birds and
other animals. When it finds an animal, it gets
very still. The dog will point at the animal with
its nose! That way, the hunter knows where
the bird or animal is hiding.

Goldens Helping People

Goldens are good **service dogs**. They help people in wheelchairs. They also make good **guide dogs**. Guide dogs lead people who cannot see. Goldens stay calm when they are working. They like to do what they have been trained for.

Fast Fact

Golden retrievers make great therapy dogs – they help make unwell people feel better.

Goldens are also good **search and rescue dogs**. They help find people who are lost or injured. They find people trapped under snow or under buildings that have fallen down.

Fast Fact

Search and rescue dogs are used all around the world.

Best of the Breed

In 2003, a Golden named Orca saved his owner's life. Orca's owner's wheelchair fell into a ditch. She fell out of the chair and into a stream. Orca ran for help. He brought someone to save his owner.

Fast Fact

Orca won an award in England for saving his owner.

In 2001, two tall buildings in New York City collapsed after jet planes crashed into them. Search and rescue dogs looked for people who were trapped there. They barked when they found someone. Many of these dogs were Golden Retrievers.

Fast Fact

Goldens named Riley, Woody, Thunder, Ana, Harley, and Dusty searched for people in New York City. They were true heroes!

Glossary

Cheetah – a large, very fast member of the cat family that lives in Africa and Asia

Coat – an animal's hair or fur

Devoted – loving and loyal

Dog park – a park meant for dogs, where they can run and play

Fetch – a game played by throwing something for a dog to retrieve

Guide dog – a dog trained to help someone who cannot see

Leash – a strap, usually attached to a collar or harness, to help control a dog being taken for a walk

Litter – A group of puppies born to the same mother at the same time

Loyal – faithful

Newborn – any animal that was born within the past few days

Nursing – drinking milk from a mother's breast

Police dog – a dog trained to help police look for drugs, explosives, or other things

Retriever – a dog trained to bring an item back to the dog's owner

Search and rescue dog – a dog trained to search for lost people

Service dog – a dog trained to help a person who cannot hear or who is in a wheelchair

Training – teaching

Undercoat – thick, fuzzy hair that grows under a dog's outer coat during the winter, to help the dog keep warm

Index